To Us, All Flowers Are Roses

T0287980

To Us, All Flowers Are Roses

Poems by
Lorna Goodison

University of Illinois Press
Urbana and Chicago

This book is printed on acid-free paper.

Library of Congress Cataloging-in-Publication Data
Goodison, Lorna
To us, all flowers are roses : poems / by Lorna Goodison.
p.   cm.
ISBN 10: 0-252-06459-3 (pbk.)
ISBN 13: 978-0-252-06459-3
1. Caribbean Area—Poetry. I. Title.
PR9265.9.G6T61995
811—dc20   94-31978
CIP

To John Edward Chamberlin

Acknowledgments

Grateful acknowledgment is made
of the following publications in which
some of these poems previously appeared:

The Hudson Review

Saturday Night

Nimrod

The Literary Review

Caribbean Quarterly

Wasafiri

Kyk-Over-Al

Jamaica Journal

Litera Pur

Contents

To Us, All Flowers Are Roses

Missing the Mountains

For years I called the Blue Mountains home.
I spent my days faceting poems from rockstones.
By moonshine I polished them, they flashed fire like true gems.

I was included then in all the views of the mountains.
The hand that flung me down to the plains
was powered by the wrath of hurricanes.

Now from the flat lands of Liguanea
I view the mountains with strict detachment.
I remark upon their range and harmony of blues.

Respect due to their majesty, I keep my distance.
I must now carry proof of my past existence
in the form of one blue stone mined near mountain heart.

I show too a wildness, an intensity
drawn from the mountains' energy.
This is a request to all left behind me.

Bury me up there in the high blue mountains
and I promise that this time I will return to teach the wind
how to make poetry from tossed about and restless leaves.

October in the Kingdom of the Poor

October, month for rainy weather.
The evening sky above thick and purple,
at its heart hidden a white and watery moon.

And i wonder, is so six o'clock stay everywhere?
Like in that place in West Africa
where i come from as a child?

Where massa come from, is so it stay too?
And one mind say i wonder too much,
wonder . . . about things that have no answer.

Sometimes when i am standing, wondering
under an October sky, purple
like the royal robes of King Solomon,

a taffeta rain-streaked lavender-purple sky
like the wide skirts of queen elizabeth's dress,
sprinkled with stars silver and spaced

so that you can count them . . .
sometimes if i stand quite still,
the sky just drapes itself around my shoulders

and i stand robed, royal in the kingdom of the poor.
And then,
the stars just come and encircle my head
in a gracious diadem.

Birth Stone

The older women wise and tell Anna
first time baby mother,
"hold a stone upon your head and follow
a straight line go home."

For like how Anna was working in the
field, grassweeder
right up till the appointed hour
that the baby was to come.

Right up till the appointed hour
when her clear heraldic water
broke free and washed her down.

Dry birth for you young mother;
the distance between the field and home
come in like the Gobi desert now.
But your first baby must born abed.

Put the woman stone on your head
and walk through no man's land
go home. When you walk, the stone
and not you yet, will bear down.

Mother, the Great Stones Got to Move

Mother, one stone is wedged across the hole in our history
and sealed with blood wax.
In this hole is our side of the story, exact figures,
headcounts, burial artifacts, documents, lists, maps
showing our way up through the stars; lockets of brass
containing all textures of hair clippings.
It is the half that has never been told,
and some of us must tell it.

Mother, there is the stone on the hearts of some women and men
something like an onyx, cabochon-cut,
which hung on the wearer seeds bad dreams. Speaking for the small
dreamers of this earth, plagued with nightmares, yearning
for healing dreams
we want the stone to move.

Upon an evening like this, mother, when one year is making way
for another, in a ceremony attended by a show of silver stars,
mothers see the moon, milk-fed, herself a nursing mother
and we think of our children and the stones upon their future
and we want these stones to move.

For the year going out came in fat at first
but toward the harvest it grew lean,
and many mouth corners gathered white
and another kind of poison, powdered white
was brought in to replace what was green.
And death sells it with one hand
and with the other death palms a gun
then death gets death's picture
in the papers asking

"where does all this death come from?"
Mother, stones are pillows
for the homeless sleep on concrete sheets.
Stone flavors soup, stone is now meat,

the hard-hearted giving our children
stones to eat.

Mother, the great stones over mankind got to move.
It's been ten thousand years we've been watching them now
from various points in the universe.
From the time of our birth as points of light
in the eternal coiled workings of the cosmos.
Roll away stone of poisoned powders come
to blot out the hope of our young.
Move stone of sacrificial lives we breed
to feed to suicide god of tribalism.
From across the pathway to mount morning
site of the rose quartz fountain
brimming anise and star water
bright fragrant for our children's future
Mother these great stones got to move.

Coir

Then, the mattress was a pallet stuffed with coir
and after a rough quota of say six hundred nights
of good dreams like pumpkin and cho cho—(new life)
pretty water—(prosperity), excrement—(money), and say
114 bad dreams of wedding—(funeral), old house
missing teeth—(death), or cats—(enemy)
the coir would feel it had taken enough pressure
and would send out vengeful needles
to bore cruelly into the skin.

Rassy our mattress man was a "beardman" who bore
a resemblance to the monk Rasputin.
He favored garments in the color of dusk
and if his head was bent over and the light was sloping
toward evening, you could imagine him in a monk's cell,
telling beads against the next phase of his life
which would find him in control of a Tzarina.
He had one eye walled off to the public
but I could see through that curtain
the worship hidden there for my mother.

But of what use were such feelings?
He was content to receive a meal at noon from her hands
and tremble gratefully at the thought of her pointed fingers
peeling moon-white Lucea yams and seasoning meat
so that you smelled her hand;
that is, a benediction of spices would rise up
to cover you when you entered through her gates.
His movements are slow,
dark molasses is his infrequent speech.
He can sit still for what seems to a fidgety child
like 999 hours.

But something stirs his slow self into speeded up action
when Rassy whips the coir.

First he folds his handkerchief into half, three points,
a triangle, a mask. He ties it round the lower half of his face,
pulls down his cap to just above his eyes.
Then he runs his thumb and forefinger
along the thick wire of his whip.
The handle too is of wire but padded with cloth over and over.
Ready, he approaches the red unruly mass
spilled from its ripped open ticking case.
He approaches the small red mountain, muttering
some ancient incantation to protect him from fierce fiber.
His arm jerks back and flicks forward, he delivers the first
blow, the coir registers receival of whipping
by sending out a cloud of frightened red dust.
When Rassy whips the rebellious coir he whips
all his enemies, exorcizes life pain and causes rain
to fall down red from what he sends up to the heavens.

The woman who threw the acid that coagulated his eye
first rain of blows.
Then the colonial Government, the Governor and Queen Victoria
for sending that heartless facety letter commending
ex-slaves to "industry, thrift, and obedience"
when the people were just rightly asking for justice,
and land to live on and grow food.
The first man who had the idea to leave and go
to Africa and interfere with the people who were minding
their own business, a hard rain of blows.
For Mussolini and the Italian Army
on behalf of Haile Selassie, five straight minutes of blows.
To Babylon in general for generic evil, hunger, disease
bad minded people, Rassy rains blows.
He whips them all for a good part of the morning
red clouds about his head flying frightened vapor from his whip.
And when the coir has been beaten into submission
he walks away triumphant, sweating, removes the mask
and wipes his eyes, it comes away red but his blood
is running free.

[7]

He asks of my mother, a cool drink
of water which he sips with the air of a victorious warrior
before he settles at the machine to stitch
the big square of new striped ticking
into which he will imprison the chastened coir.

Elephant

Memory claims that in a jungle once,
a great mother elephant, crazed
with grief for her lost son,
wrapped her trunk around a baobab tree
and wrenched it free from its upside down
hold in the earth and trumpeted down
the hole in the earth for her vanished one.

Elephant, the lost the cursed one lumbers
up from under the big trees in Queen Victoria's park.
This man more pachyderm than man, skin draped loose,
grey, muddy as tarpaulin, over swollen elephantiasis limbs.
He moves bent over, weighed by the bag of crosses
over his shoulder, his lips droop tubular.
Small children appear and chant, "elephant, elephant, . . ."

He rears back on his huge hind legs trumpeting
threats of illegal surgery by broken glass bottle,
death to small children, who scatter before him like antelopes
and elands, skittering across the asphalt heading home.
Elephant, loneliest one in all creation, your friends
the night grazing mules, tethered by dark hills of coal
in Mullings grass yard.

Poor Elephant always walking
hoping one day he would turn a corner and come upon
a clearing familiar to long memory,
wide green space and baobab trees.
For there his mother and the great herds would be, free.

Bag-a-Wire

Sir, if you see Bag-a-wire walking
into the furnace of the sun at evening
can you please direct him down to Race Course?

For there he will find Marcus Garvey
the only man possessing appropriate pardon
to free him from his long and living death.

Man, if you are the one to direct him,
make sure you tell him loudly, for all his senses
are now concentrated into a laserlike stare.

A stare he trains up and down the frame
of every passing man, black, heavy-set
inclining to be pompous but majestic, giant

of a far sighted man and prophet who could be
Marcus Garvey. Prophets speak light and this one
has the luminous oratory which, dissolving dark,

could finally set Bag-a-wire free.
For when he sees him finally (a scene he has played
in his mind often) he will kneel so contrite:

on the government sidewalk a fallen knight kneels
and puts his forehead to the shoe of the visionary
whom he sold for food, saying "Sir, I beg your pardon

I am related by hard design and infamy
to a line of betrayers without whom saviors
can never fulfil their shining destiny . . ."

Bun Down Cross Roads

Bun Down Cross Roads, ex-esquire, former gentleman
of substance and shopkeeper.
Now convicted arsonist and fruit seller.
Special purveyor of heavy-jowled governor mango
and scowling coarse skinned ugli fruit.

Bun Down could concoct in ripe and fruity tones
unique and extravagant combinations
of forty shilling words and never repeat
a particular formation once, in the distance
between King Street and Cross Roads.

Legend of Bun Down, bad word merchant, goes
he is arrested, brought before her majesty's court
for using decent language, indecently.
Bun Down is fined for one forty shilling word.
And in a gesture befitting his better days,

thrust his hand deep down into the pocket
of his rusty black serge suit and extracts
a crisp and freshly inked ten pound note.
It crackles in the courtroom air and Bun Down
rolls his baritone providing rich timbre, under.

"I have on my person these ten pounds, I wish
to curse, until I have reached this sum."

And so said, so it was done.

Papacita

Sweet boy sonny
had not worked for years.
Everyday he just got up
to sit down and pose
endless mutiple-eyed
dominoes with Papacita.
Papacita with the gold-shielded teeth.

Papacita who always favored a clean merino
over any shirt with collar and sleeves.
Papacita whose hair was pomaded
to lie down under the thigh top
of a woman's silk stocking.
Papacita who never had to work again
because he spent one lifetime

cutting hectares of cane in Cuba.
Papacita, who my brother Keith said
had a trunk full of money under his trunk bed.
When Papacita's memory was pierced
by one dagger, two dagger, three dagger rum,
he would habla loquacious of hard work,
sin, and rum in Havana, before Fidel and Che rode into town.

In City Gardens Grow No Roses as We Know Them

Outside the street ran hard
a still dark river of asphalt.
At the core of the many-celled tenement
lay the central brick-paved courtyard
severe square of unyielding red soil
for the only tree in one hundred and seventeen
Orange Street.

The long blunted silver trunk
of a decapitated breadfruit tree
beheaded by a blind flying sheet
of zinc driven by a hurricane's fury.
Still the tree refused to die completely
but stood leaning forward to the East
as if hoping to receive something regenerative.

A thick crown of new leaves/antlers of branches,
blossoms that bud into brown swords
fruit like green globes, scale-backed dripping staining sap
tasting like fresh baked bread after
its white dense flesh has passed through fire.
The only tree, half alive in 117 Orange Street
standing headless defiant and hoping.

Awaiting a last fruitfulness, a new life and greening
paying obeisance at the site of the sun's religious rising.
And the people planted what they could.
In paved yards with no lawns they planted.
In discarded paint pans that they filled
with fertile soil they transported in bags
from the green growing yards of St. Andrew.

In St. Andrew's houses they worked as maids
as nurses to small children calling big women
by their first names. Big women who called children
miss or mister, or young missus or young massa.

They worked as yard boys even when
they were shuffling work worn old men.

They were cooks in the kitchens of gracious homes
who cooked their meals outside on coal pot stoves.
The second cooking after the big house dinner
was the twilight cooking of provender
rank salted fish and offal, tuberous ground provisions,
the food of slavery, unfit for high tables.
Food that smelled like sweat and strong seasoning

with the musk fragrance of coconut oil pervading
the dusk outside the big house, they ate
from enamel or tin plates, cheap utensils set aside
for the exclusive use of yardboys and maids.
Bent forks dull knives of base metal
and for the belly-wash, sangaree of poor people,
a tin can with a soldered on kimbo of a handle.

Sometimes though like Lazarus they got what was left
from the tables of the people with plenty.
They carried it home in bags, the good earth
like loose dark fruitcake, alluvial gold,
rich soil from the yards of plenty
for the paint pan gardens in the paved yards
of the poor who lived in the city.

They planted mint first, spiked lancelike leaves
of black mint, fragrant light green peppermint.
Mint tea, necessary for the soothing of stomachs,
cure all to bad feeling and nonspecific discomforts.
Mint for the benediction its leaves exuded
when the early morning breezes moved away
from the side of the sea and passed through dense places.

Breezes like kind overseers or benign landlords
or land missus inspecting rented places.
Maybe they planted mint as a green barometer
for that is how you would know if angels passed,

[14]

when the mint plants would shudder and send out
their sweet sharp mint fragrance.
After all, everyone knows that when angels pass

through noisy crowds everyone falls suddenly silent.
Maybe then mint is the scent of angels.
Source of divine perfume with dark sharp base notes
rising up to tender green top notes
distilled to become essential oil of fresh annointing.
Planted strategically outside the welcoming doors
to measure the movement of angels.

Occasionally, an old chamber pot
would be transformed, pressed into higher service.
Battered and used, fallen into black holes
dark cavities eaten into its white enamel surface
it would become cleansed from years of low service
brought out from its shadow dwelling of nocturnal shame
and elevated to the level of respectable receptacle.

Necessary medicinal herbs, flowers easy to grow
no delicate blooms could survive here.
In city gardens grow no roses as we know them.
So the people took the name and bestowed it
generic, on all flowers, called them roses.
So here we speak a litany of the roses that grow
in the paint-pan chamber-pot gardens of Kingston.

See the quick growing four-o'-clock
that sleeps all days and springs suddenly up
in the afternoon, comes wide awake as if
it is the emblem of factory workers
pulling a round of the night shift.

Bright carmine pucker of bachelor buttons
for wild men who will not marry.

Dangling furry fall of puss tail,
Sansivira or Donkey's ears,

the tuneful Monkey fiddle.
Perfect plants for yards where tyrannical landlords
allow no animals.

And all gardens then contained the necessary
the precious and bitter carminative cactus plant and flower
of the aloe and the tuna.
For the restoration of lost shining.
It coats the insides and the hair and skin
with a healing shine that by some botanical alchemy
leaves behind a kind of glow.
The afterglow of the aloes experience
is a kind of halo.

The croton with its varicolored self
prefiguring abstract paintings
creating wild eccentric patterns
in multiple and riotous colors.

And the Coleus. Say its name
with reverence devout.
Say it in the ordinary tongue
call it Joseph's coat
after the splendid garment
bestowed on the dreamer
by his father.

And Joseph must be the patron saint
of poets of the city
survivors of stabbings, murder, and treachery
compelled always to interpret the dreams
the visions of lovers, paupers, beggars, kings.

Renewed, renewed by the angel smell of mint.
Lulled to sleep by the running stream of traffic,
walking by the dark asphalt river,
divining images from hard unyielding surfaces.

Witnessing, witnessing in crowded places.
Praying in spite of, nonetheless.
In hanging gardens in paint cans
in Babylon.

Losing their heads and praying for new life.

Weaving the patched coats of Joseph.

Fabulous lost and found again
unfraying at the selvages.

In the face of terrors witnessing
through plagues, wars, and imprisonings.

In tenements and walled places
marking how blood spilled leaves shadows.

And the smell of fear is a harsh perfume
city dwellers wear and are used to.

But the poet offspring of Joseph
have no choice but to sing.

To dream and interpret
reminding the righteous
of the blessing active in angels' wings
which releases the smell of mint.

And leaves behind the unseen
mark upon your door.

After angels assigned to city dwellers
have come and gone
passed over.

Songs of the Fruits
and Sweets of Childhood

O small and squat
with thin tough skin
containing the slick flesh
of mackafat
which makes fillings
like putty between
the teeth.

Cream pink pomander
like a lady's sachet
is the genteel roseapple
scenting the breath.

Jade green lantern
light astringent
is the tart taste
of the jimbelin.

Tough skinnned
brown pods
of stinking toe
you broke open hard
upon stone
to free the pungent
dry powdery musk
called by some,
locust.

A brittle sweet cup
brims
with a sweetish slime
in which
tiny grey-eyed seeds
seem to wink.

And coolie plums
and red/yellow
coat plums
and plums called
for June time
and apples
O taheti.

But of all fruit
the most perfect is
the dark ocher
taste like rosewater
color like logwood honey
that is a naseberry.

The starapple
wears a thick coat
of royal purple
and at its center
sports a star
of many points.

This is a lover's fruit
because it runs
with a sweet
staining milk
and the flesh
if bitten too deep,
has been known to bind you.

Of the sweets
the sweets
now sing,
beginning with the sour
fleshed tamarind.

Which if rolled
into sugar
becomes balanced

into being
the yin and yang
of sweets.

A soft brown square
of rare delight
is a wedge
of guava cheese.
O guava cheese
make you sneeze.
Penny a cut
full yu gut?

And in singing
the lungs will fill
with the sweet dust
of corn,
pounded, parched
blended with
cane sugar
to tickle the
channels of breathing.
Inhale, sneeze
sing so
"Asham O."

The rise
of the palette's roof
is a nice height
under which
to tuck the pink backed
paradise plum.
Its smooth
white underbelly
melting level
with the tongue.

A mint ball
is divided by thin

varicolored stripes
like the porcelain
marble of a prince.

A shaggy
grater cake
can be rich brown
if it takes
its color
from burnt sugar.

But if it holds
its coconut milk
to itself
and mixes only
with white sugar,
it becomes
what some consider
a greater cake.
It is then topped
with a show off hat
of cochineal or magenta.

A Bustamante backbone
is a stubborn mixture
of coconut
and caramelized sugar.
One side wears
a thin skin
of grease proof paper
which you peel off
before chewing.

Hard on the jawbone
it is,
tying up the teeth.

But the tie-teeth
is another kind

of sweet.
Tangled and sweet
like some things
tempting
but so tangled.

Hot pink
stretcher
like a fuschia lipstick.

Whole peanuts
suspended
in crystalized sugar
is a wangla.

And the ring game
or join up
of pink top
candy bump
going round and round
in a ring
of the fruits and sweets
of childhood
sing.

Outside the Gates

Outside the high gates of the school
named for all the saints
gathered each day a band of good women
seeking a steady and righteous living
through purveying food to children.

These women in the service of children
after a time became like saints.
Their heads surrounded by straw halos
of golden Jippi-Jappa weave
through which the honey colored sun streamed.

They sold fruits and sweets from wide baskets
balanced on upturned carton boxes,
and baked goods that they displayed
in small cabinets called showcases
with transparent gleaming glass windows.

The fruits were colored like edible jewels,
the sweets did not originate in anonymous factories,
each sweet had its own shape
stamped with its maker's hand,
each sweet was an original then.

All kind women, except for one
whom it is said had lost all her children.
We were warned to avoid her, to resist
her bitter wares, her wiles, her witch-way
of enticing small children to enter

their names into her dirty exercise book
of credit. For once their names were marked down
she would anxiously wait for them to falter
in their small debt repayment.
She was known to take great pleasure

in entering classrooms and pointing
with a crooked finger at the poor cringing debtor
who would then be punished severely
by a principled teacher, warning against
the terrible practice of crediting.

But the teacher's punishment
would become as nothing
compared to the humiliation
for days, of your classmates chanting
"yay, yay, you trust and don't pay."

To be avoided too was Miss Gladys
the queen of the Ptomaine Palace,
her flat fritters laying drowsy
with sleeping overnight oil.
They slumbered in her show case unaware

that there were terrible rumors
about their function as mattresses
for prehistoric drummer roaches
and that her soft topped puddings
were concocted with disgusting ingredients.

Every child in the school denied
ever having given her patronage,
although she sold her greasy foodstuff
at those gates for many years,
standing near to the magician snowball man.

His painted cart a bright chariot
scarlet red with fiery wheels
and stippled with millions
of hundreds and thousands varicolored
confetti dots and transparent streamers blowing.

The ice of his trade was contained and covered within
the carefully zinc-lined stomach.
He was a skilled ventriloquist

and a puppet master, with a doll through which
he spoke to you, for a copper willy-penny.

He created his own aerated water
in magical fantastic colors.
A lurid lime, a straw dye red
and the favorite of all children,
O the invisible cream soda.

To create snowballs, he would shave
the ice with a shiny metal wedge
which rasped over the frozen surface
until it had ingested
enough ice crystals to be pressed

into a round snowball which was then
drenched with cherry red or citron gold syrup.
Securely standing in round-fitted holes
the long-necked bottles of bright syrup rode
on display in the open shelves of the chariot.

Snow balls with syrup, an everyday treat,
Snowballs crowned with soapy ice cream
became "back and front," every child's dream.
While around it all bounced amber and chocolate
striped bees in a sugary bumbling dance.

Concert

Brother Kingsley had the swiftest legs,
they would move like sharpened blades
cutting through finishing line tapes
on sports days when we would receive
for prizes, dictionaries and holy Bibles.

He was a dancer, could split, snap-fall,
boogie, gallows, and shuffle better
than any other boy who called himself dancer.
As soon as his heels touched ground
they would lift up again, pushing against
slow air, seeking to align themselves
with the fastest moving currents in the atmosphere.

At the talent show, we were sure he'd win.
The entire school was behind him, cheering
his every turn, split and spin, he was winning
till he affected a clutching movement he had seen
the older men practice.

Miss Stirling judged that move
too adult and dangerous to youth.
She awarded the prize to a girl
who rattled out, with nervous pebbles
in her mouth, a dull unburnished memory gem.

Dressed as she was in a drooping slipper-satin
christian-quattie dress, we booed the results
of this unfair contest and spoke for years
of how they robbed him.

Annie Pengelly

I come to represent the case
of one Annie Pengelly,
maidservant, late of the San Fleming Estate
situated in the westerly parish of Hanover.

Hanover, where that masif
mountain range
assumes the shape of a Dolphin's head
rearing up in the blue expanse overhead
restless white clouds round it foaming.

Those at sea would look up
and behold, mirrored, a seascape in the sky.

It is this need to recreate,
to run 'gainst things, that cause
all this confusion.

The same need that made men
leave one side of the world
to journey in long, mawed ships,
to drogue millions of souls
to a world
that they call the new one
in competition with the original act
the creation of the old one.

So now you are telling me to proceed
and proceed swiftly.
Why have I come here representing Annie?

Well this is the first thing she asked me to say,
that Annie is not even her real name.
A name is the first thing we own in this world.

We lay claim to a group of sounds
which rise up and down and mark out our space
in the air around us.
We become owners of a harmony of vowels and consonants
singing a specific meaning.

Her real name was given to her
at the pastoral ceremony of her outdooring.
Its outer meaning was, "she who is precious to us."

It had too a hidden part, a kept secret.
A meaning known only to those within
the circle of her family.

For sale Bidderman, one small girl,
one small African girl answering now
to the name of Annie.

Oh Missus my dear, when you write Lady Nugent
to tell her of your splendid birthday
of the ivory moire gown you wore
that you send clear to London for.

You can tell her too how you had built for you
a pair of soft, supple leather riding boots
fashioned from your own last
by George O'Brian Wilson
late of Aberdeen
now Shoemaker and Sadler of Lucea, Hanover
late occupation,
bruk Sailor.

One pair of tortoiseshell combs,
one scrolled silver backed mirror,
one dinner party where they killed
one whole cow
with oaken casks of Madeira wine
to wash it down.

And don't forget, one small African girl,
answering now to the name of Annie.

With all that birthday show of affection
Massa never sleep with missus.
But I am not here to talk about that,
that is backra business.

I am really here just representing Annie Pengelly.

For Missus began to make Annie
sleep across her feet
come December when northers began to blow.

Northers being the chill wheeling tail end
of the winter breezes
dropping off their cold what lef' in Jamaica
to confuse the transplanted Planter.

Causing them to remember words like "hoarfrost" and "moors"
from a frozen vocabulary they no longer
had use for.

When this false winter breeze would
careen across canefields
Missus would make Annie lie draped,
heaped across her feet
a human blanket
nothing covering her as she gave
her warmth to Missus.

So I come to say that History owes Annie
the brightest woolen blanket.
She is owed too, at least twelve years of sleep
stretched out,
free to assume the stages of sleep
flat on her back,
or profiled like the characters
in an Egyptian frieze.

Most nights though, Missus don't sleep.
And as Annie was subject to Missus will,
Annie was not to sleep as long
as Missus kept her open-eyed vigil.

Sometimes Missus sit up
sipping wine from a cut glass goblet.
Talking, talking.

Sometimes Missus dance and sing
like she was on a stage,
sad cantatrice solo
on a stage performing.

At the end of her performance
she would demand that Annie clap
clap loud and shout "encore."

Encouraged by this she would sing
and dance on,
her half-crazed torch song of rejection.

Sometimes Annie nod off,
Missus jook her with a pearl-tipped pin.
Sometimes Annie tumble off the chair
felled by sleep.
Missus slap her awake again.
Then in order to keep her alert, awake
she devised the paper torture.

One pile of newspapers
a sharp pair of scissors later,
Annie learned about
the cruel make-work task
that is the *cut-up*
to throw-away of old newspaper.

For if Missus could not sleep
Annie gal you don't sleep that night,
and poor Missus enslaved by love
fighting her servitude with spite.

So I say history owes Annie
thousands of nights
of sleep upon a feather bed.
Soft feathers from the breast of
a free, soaring bird,
one bright blanket,
and her name returned,
she who is precious to us.

Annie Pengelly O.
I say, History owe you.

Nayga Bikkle

Yes sir, massa was always complaining about our cooking.
Massa called it "Coarse Cuisine."
Somehow it downright seemed to offend him
whenever nayga cooking.

"Nayga Bikkle O," all manner of ground provision.
Sing now of the tuberous diversity of yam
from different race and country.

Firm and strong, the negro yam, smooth the snow white yam.
The subtle eating chinee yam, the powdery golden yellow yam,
the aristocrat of yam the Lucea yam. Small island yam,
St. Vincent yam, miniature yam, the yampie. They even have
that nice soft yam, named for the sweetness of the woman.

What could possibly be more pleasing than a hot steaming slice
of dry powdery yam protected by a salt ting watch man
and floating in a fragrant sea of plenty coconut oil?

Ah the rich, gold-fleshed pumpkin with the secret spring within the
    belly,
pointed okra pods that slide across the tongue.
The generosity of the quick growing calalloo, verdant, season up,
and steamed down.

And these are only some of the wonders of nayga bikkle.

One day in the middle of October
month for rainy weather,
as God would have it here comes massa,
master of all him survey.

One minute he was outlined against the sky
luminous in the afternoon light
which was gold and gilding his hair and skin.
The buttons upon his jacket brass and blazing.

[32]

The metal trim upon his saddle joined in the
blazing too,
till massa was beginning to seem like him was more than man,
him was taller than a cedar tree
more lofty than Blue Mountain Peak.

When the sky suddenly frown and get dark.
And in this darkness overwhelming
massa shining was suddenly dimmed.

The rain started to pour, no advance drizzle
just a big thunder clap
and the sky opened up.
The nearest place of shelter
was my little wattle and daub hut.

I say "good evening" when massa come in.

Massa grunt two times for an answer
then him stand there growling
by the door way,
growling to outmatch the thunder.

Well sir, to think that massa could fall so low
as to have to take up shelter in my humble abode.
But the rain was falling like it had no plan for stopping.

Now as it so happens I was eating my dinner,
and what else could a poor person like me
be dining upon except coarse cuisine?

The said cuisine, that massa find so downright
offending.
And you know as I sit there I suddenly see the smells
rise up like strong spirits out of my pot
rise up and start to worry him.

Well, I was eating my dinner,
I have manners, I share a plate for massa.

[33]

When I eat, I want to sleep!
I close my eyes and when I wake, massa was gone
so was the food in the plate.

Tell anyone that I tell you that massa eat nayga bikkle.

And you know it never kill him, for him live long
and make plenty man fret,
but till the day he dead he would never truly say
that him never eat nayga bikkle yet.

Nayga Bikkle o, the integration of rices and peas,

red peas and rice or the peas of the congo that in the course of their
    transplantation
were transformed into gungoo.

The pretty little black and white black-eyed peas.
As a matter of fact, we call all beans—peas.
It's a generic tribute to the protein filled legume

that is so much a foundation stone in the architecture of nayga
    bikkle.
All peas come together with rice joined by the ubiquitous kindness
    of coconut milk,
which gives to food a texture, like silk upon the tongue.

Ah, the wonders of the salted cod fish, making tasteful intervention
in every poor somebody's dish, fried lacelike in a fritter,
mated equally with the yellow aril of the ackee.
Such cooking claims the air, its strong seasoning
drawing mouth water in anticipation of high feasting.

Behold how good and pleasant it is to taste the food
the bounty born of the plenty of our poverty.
The nayga bikkle of this land, season strong
you smell we hand?
O the wonders of Nayga Bikkle.

Inna Calabash

Inna calabash
Inna calabash
tell them that the baby
that count in them census already
Inna calabash

One slave child
that count already
while it inside my belly
tell them that the baby
Inna calabash.

She show me
Quasheba show me one day
when I faint in the field of cane

When I cry and say
Why I can't be like missus
siddown and plait sand
and throw stone after breeze.

Quasheba show me
how the calabash contained
for a slave gal like me
a little soft life and ease.

Pick a big calabash
bore both ends she say
shake out the gray pulp belly.
Run a string through both ends
and tie it across your belly.

Drop the little shift frock
make outta Massa
coarse oznaburg cloth
over your calabash belly

Nothing Massa like
like more slave pickney
to grow into big slave
to serve slavery.

You will get rest
when you have belly.
When you rest enough
just take it off.

Say you fall
say you lose baby.
Quasheba show me
all I need to know.
Inna calabash.

Name Change: Morant Bay Uprising

After the trouble
some with the name Bogle
catch fraid like sickness
and take panic for the cure.

For it was going to be hard to survive
if identified with the hung figure
revolving in the wind
from the yard arm of the Wolverine.

So some took bush for it
and swallow cerasee to cleanse
deacon Paul blessed name
from blood and memory.

Or some with the help of bamboo root
bend the truth into Bogie, or Boggis,
or Buddle, or some come out of that
alphabet altogether.

Some would answer to no name on earth.
Sometimes after man see hanging
as example, preach like Paul,
your words will fall on stony ground.

Ground Doves

Small querulous birds
feathers like swatches of earth
graced with wings,
opt for walking.

The female ones
sport surprising underslips
trimmed with stunning passementerie.
Braided arabesques

scalloping round their hems
but that is rarely shown, except
when they bend to scramble
for stale bread crumbs

they have come to expect as due.
Ground doves make you uneasy
because there was a time
when you too walked

and saved your wings
and would not reach high
for the sweet risk
inside the lips of hibiscus

but saved your wings,
and scrambled for used bread
and left over things . . .

White Birds

At first, we liked to describe them
as doves.
The white pigeons who came to live
at this house.
Appearing first as a circle with wings,
then some blessing pulled the circle in,
so that its center became our house.
Now in these eaves
a benediction of birds.
Their nervous hearts
in sync enough
with our rhythms
they enter into this house.
So sometimes in the middle
of doing some woman's thing
I look up to find us
in a new painting.
House in a rock
with wooden floors
a boy and white pigeons.

From the Garden of the Women Once Fallen

Thyme

Woman alone, living
in a tenement of enmity.
One room of back-biting
standpipe flowing strife.

Recall one dry Sunday
of no rice and peas no meat
how you boiled a handful
of fresh green thyme

to carry the smell of Sunday
as usual.
Thyme, herb of contraction
rising as steaming incense
of save-face.

When you dwell among enemies
you never make them salt your pot.
You never make them know
your want.

Of Bitterness Herbs

You knotted the spite blooms into a bouquet-garni
to flavor stock for sour soups and confusion stews.
Now no one will dine with you.

A diet of bitterness is self consuming. Such herbs
are best destroyed, rooted out from the garden
of the necessary even preordained past.

Bitter herbs grow luxuriant where the grudgeful crow
dropped its shadow, starting a compost heap of need in you
to spray malicious toxins over all flowers in our rose gardens.

Bitterness herbs bake bad-minded bread, are good for little
except pickling green-eyed gall stones, then eaten alone
from wooden spoons of must-suck-salt.

In the Time of Late-Blooming Pumpkins

In this garden, water walks
and water walking enters
belly of pumpkin.

This means you are growing
big from within, all ripeness,
though somebody (Jeremiah?)

shouts from outside the garden wall
"You are all conceived in sin"
but that is just some false prophet

negative and bad mouthing.
For in this new garden
of fresh start over

with its mysteries of walking water,
give thanks for late summer's
rose afternoons shading
into amethyst, then deepening
into red water grass evenings,
time of late blooming pumpkins.

The River Wanted Out

Things are changing this side of the forest.
The river is ostriching into the sand
leaving dense stones to mark its place.
The crayfish grow thick flattened shells
and imitate land turtles.

The bulrushes, wild-haired and long limbed
when asked if they will remain
to remind us that here passed a river,
shake their locks till they blur and shriek
"We're going to be palm trees in the King's garden."

Now nobody will see their faces in this water mirror.
The ticki ticki will have no riverbottom
to shield them from the long lances of May rains.
But the worst fate of all will befall river Mumma.
She, stunning except for her scaly thighs and legs,

she who looked fine in the setting of the river,
will now have to land on her feet and learn walking,
a task requiring division of herself.
And when she walks like any ordinary woman,
she will have to sell her gold comb to buy unguents.

Unguents to smooth her scaly skin
in order to gain flat earth acceptance.
First the gold comb, then maybe herself,
the worst fate of all will befall the river Mumma
all because the river wanted out.

The Prophet Jeremiah Speaks

Today I will not speak.
I shall take these warnings
born to me as loud visions
and I shall cover them
till they do not breathe.

For they hate the sight
of me, these people.
When I appear in the marketplace
they see indigo rays stream
from my mouth, they hear

high-pitched prophecy
shatter their careful illusions.
But still God bids me show them
the poor. (I saw a man last
Thursday fight another human

for the right to eat, from a bag
of garbage outside a health
food shop. Did nobody else
see anything unusual in that?)

When I appear in the marketplace
everyone remembers some urgent
task left undone, all because
I am charged to speak. But what is worse
if I do not prophesy
God contends with me,

turns up a high-marrow deep
flame, sealed fire then
shut up burning in my bones.
I did not choose prophecy,
prophecy chose me, laid hands

on me from my youth, bid me
speak these warning words.
I am young I desire to marry,
father children and feed them
kind words, the bread of love

and no damnation! I would have
a warm soft woman as wife.
The same place to rest my head
each night and to plant the field
that I have bought. Instead I'm

used hard. Commanded to tell them
what they do not wish to know.
When they see me coming
I fear they would stone me.

So today I will not
speak. I'll seal my mouth.
At least until the high fire
within forces these hot
scorching warnings out.

Speak of the Advent of New Light

On a night of no stars it will spark
from the friction of a homeless woman's shoe
slipping along the pavement as she stoops
to stir her evening meal of trickledown
in a paintpan over a fire of damp rubbish.

Simultaneously it will glow phosphorescent
in the cupped palms of a night fisherman
as he bends to test the waters off the bay
near surrender, the wonder of the living water
bearing footprints and currents of fresh beginnings.

And small children will come in from play
pulling like kites behind them luminous
streamers of light, infused with such colors
as never the prism of the eye has reflected.
New light succeeding dark is certain, is expected.

Mysteries

Amazing how this morning
I tilt the dark stained louvers
to slant the morning air in
and the green light of peridots
streams in and fills the room.

Maybe it's the work of the rain
kind rain cleaning the air
so that all around this hill
is the jewel glow the unstained aura
of new green and no bitterness.

No smoke which clings to or rises from
humans is anywhere this morning.
Of course it could be the Hope River
running strong after a long drink
of seven days August cloud burst rains.

Fresh river come calling bringing me my birthstone.
But that is just the top layer of my mind
always wanting explanations.
How to explain that girl we heard
in the Nameless cafe near the homeless

sleeping in Harvard Square, she sang
so unconvincingly of deprivation.
A state that she had yet to visit.
And how afterward we walked outside
as the October air was turning sharp.

We agreed then that it is pointless to sing
second hand of suffering, it sounds untrue.
It is pointless to try too hard
to penetrate the mysteries like peridots,
jewel of the lost ones, filling up my room.

And that house on the edge
of the Charles River in Cambridge.
Did we once on that last departure
see framed in the early morning
a Being of light at a Bay window?

And was that Being playing
our song of separation and reuniting
the one and the same song
upon that ivory-inlaid, that ceiling high
and splendid harp?

From the Book of Local Miracles, Largely Unrecorded

Write this truth now
of the simple faith
of my mother's friend.

Who set a pot of water
over a candlewood fire
when she knew she had no food.

And in it placed
a stone
and by it waited.

Just as the water
began to break
over the stone

enter one neighbor
with an abundance
of coconuts and ground provisions.

Then another
fresh from slaughter
offering a portion of goat's flesh.

My mother always pauses
at this point in the retelling
of the miracle

and adds to the text
"She even got oil
from the coconuts."

All that she needed
was salt.
And widows have that.

Prophets and widows,
self-replenishing
measures of meal,

never ending cruse of oil.
Bright angels appearing
to meet believers
at points of need

come again
when these women
call out for miracles.

The Lace Seller

There is a woman selling cards of lace
and loops of ribbon
inside the elbow of a downtown square.
Her mother before her sold american apples,
crisp deep white flesh, packed tight
within glowing thin red wineskins.

This woman's concerns filter up
through my dreams
when I lie bathed and folded in clean sheets,
for she lies on one thin hot sheet, bed pushed
up against the door for fear of "kick-down"
and always she sleeps lightly.

This woman has a son (so do I)
except it was the police who kicked her door down
letting the thick night in, seizing him.
Lace money cannot stretch to pay Lawyer.
When I think of her son,
Lord please cover the head of my own.

The Woman Speaks to the Man
Who Has Employed Her Son

Her son was first made known to her
as a sense of unease, a need to cry
for little reasons and a metallic tide
rising in her mouth each morning.
Such signs made her know
that she was not alone in her body.
She carried him full term
tight up under her heart.

She carried him like the poor
carry hope, hope you get a break
or a visa, hope one child go through
and remember you. He had no father.
The man she made him with had more
like him, he was fair-minded
he treated all his children
with equal and absolute indifference.

She raised him twice, once as mother
then as father, set no ceiling
on what he could be doctor
earth healer, pilot take wings.
But now he tells her he is working
for you, that you value him so much
you give him one whole submachine gun
for him alone.

He says you are like a father to him.
She is wondering what kind of father
would give a son hot and exploding
death when he asks him for bread.
She went downtown and bought three
and one third yards of black cloth
and a deep crowned and veiled hat
for the day he draw his bloody salary.

She has no power over you and this
at the level of earth, what she has
are prayers and a mother's tears
and at knee city she uses them.
She says psalms for him
she reads psalms for you
she weeps for his soul
her eyewater covers you.

She is throwing a partner
with Judas Iscariot's mother
the thief on the left side
of the cross, his mother
is the banker, her draw though
is first and last for she still
throwing two hands as mother and father
she is prepared, she is done. Absalom.

Calling One Sweet Psalmist

—for Bob Marley

On the outskirts of Addis
this is a rider
guide to the line
of Kings passing
he is waiting to take me
I rise and go with him.

The journey is one
of seven days and seven nights
we pass through landscapes
of sheer drops
the wind in this part
of the country is spiced.

We will come finally
to the cool caves
where the herbsmen
of the healing people
have gathered new leaves
and tender shoots.

In the pearl light
will begin my healing
and they will purge
this man's flesh
of the poison
of the old ways.

Nourish me then
when all death
has been drawn from me
with liquid amber
and wild bees honey.
You I leave to marvel,

[53]

you to create burial spectacle
the whole me is moving
to another height
(calling one sweet psalmist)
I've been promised a play
off David's harp.

(Come in now one sweet psalmist)
new songs are being released
in me, I chant now
celestially, I am become
what I was born to be
I am, I am sweet psalmist.

Deep-Sea Diving

For the rare ones, the pieces only glimpsed at in dreams,
it is essential that you dive deeply.
On the surface all that you will see are objects discernable
to anybody, in colors between everyday and ordinary.
What a splendid spectrum ranges below for those
who dive deeply.

It is difficult at first, learning to breathe below water
to convert the lungs meant only for inhalation on earth.
To open the chambers of conversion situated between the lungs
and the heart.
But belief will key its doors open, amphibian, after a season
of persistent knocking.

The plunge. To take it, sometimes you cannot by yourself
just voluntarily dive.
So some hand might push you from behind and whatever the reason
behind the shove
you will live to thank the hand which might have thought
that it was sending you to your drowning.

Thank the action then, thank the hand which tipped you over
into deep diving.
Once down, you will swear that you have died.
For it goes all dark at the end of living only on surface.
Your now expanding lungs will make a high wheezing sound
as water saturates the near atrophied amphibian tissue.

In time though all your systems will settle, even your eyes
will get used to the sting of strong salt in deep water,
then you will begin to notice the blessed order there.
The government of grace which provides camouflage rocks
as sanctuaries for chosen fish.

The same grace government which can cause sharks to trip
over their menacing shadows.

[55]

But mostly it is liquid tranquility and where creation
was first conceived
and upon its floors lie treasures deep-sea divers will hereafter
take extraordinary risks for.

For today, there is no need to speak
of the treacherous scuttlefish.
Just to say that despite their balancing existence below,
do not fear to dive deeply.
It is necessary, in order to master all the levels.

And if you already know all about earth runnings,
the next logical lessons have to be in the art
of deep-sea diving.
And when that is mastered, when all that is done
the teacher will introduce you to the possibilities,
infinite possibilities of flying.

Some Things You Do Not Know about Me

When I am alone like this
I drink from a saucer,
I eat naturally with my fingers
and I never wear shoes.
For seven years I drank my morning tea
from the same cup.
It was a rich brown like bitter chocolate
and stippled with tiny white dots over its round surface
except all round the rim
where my constant drinking had washed those dots away.
I think I may have swallowed them, because some nights
I feel like a trillion small punctuation
periods are swarming inside me,
waiting to attach themselves
to the ends of my unwritten lines and sentences.
But that is not the most important thing about me.
You see, what I've never told you is that I'm really a dancer.
Yes, when I'm alone when nobody is watching
you should see me dancing.
Sometimes it's my dance of joy, like when
I'm writing a poem and somehow it's working,
I'm so happy that my feet start to pump up and down
like I'm playing a big baritone pipe organ.
My hands fly to the keys and out like I'm pulling out music notes,
and my feet, my feet are dancing.
If the poem is really coming now, straight and sure
no holding it back as it heads for its union with the page,
then I simply must take advantage and dance.
So I throw my hands up over my head
thereby releasing the poem.
And then I push the chair away
and for ten minutes or so I dance around the table.
It's a whirling kind of dance I do,
it makes my head really spin,
my particular form of dancing.
Round and round the table I go

till my wild whirling
shaves the edges off the square table,
and I'm whirling now around a round table.
I go so until I fall down,
and wherever my feet are pointed
it is there that I take the poem.
Like this one, I think now I will have to take it East,
so I will light a stick of incense
and play Bob Dylan wondering
if she might be in Tangier.
Or I just might sit quietly
and take my own self there.
All this I do before I begin the evening's cooking.
And when you come home you always find me placid, calm, normal.
And these are only some of the things
you do not know about me.

In the Mountains of the Moon, Uganda

In the mountains of the moon, Uganda
God wept fresh tears when God's gracious heart
conceived of what it would mean
for willing souls to make the journey of peril
back to Her/Him.

From these twin streams of compassion
the Nile was born.
And your soul has followed its course
winding, bending back upon itself
forcing you to bend too.

Who can walk to where the Nile begins or ends?
You with a will of iron and a head as hard.
For no one can convince you not to follow
to its ending
what God wept to create in the beginning.

Of Used-Moon Stars

The nights are glorious here.
A great indigo canopy spread overhead,
lavish needle work, heavily embroidered,
with whole moons, crescents, and stars.

Amber came to recognize the stars
made from used moons, halved,
quartered, split, and splintered
into five and seven pointed stars.

At first there is something uncertain
about them, those used-moon stars,
they hang so still and uncertain,
till the hand which split them

connects them to the source
of energy for hand-me-downs.
The stillest star then shocks out, shines forth,
certain, sure of its function in the universe.

To the Creator of All Bodies of Water
in This Instance Bays, Coves, and Harbors (From Amber)

As she rounded the Bay of St. Anthony
the blue was so cobalt
it was near unbearable.
She could taste its sea salt on the thin smooth
lining inside of her mouth.

She saw after many months
of vast burning desert,
the green cane growing.
Tall flagging lances
of veridian green, but she is off sugar.

She thinks she should let you know
that no matter what she appears to be doing
she is really designing praises
for her deliverance from the desert.
See her lying now in the Bay of St. Anthony,

her arms arranged in a sign of surrender,
the burdens of her body cast down.
She knows now that when St. Anthony sings in Spanish
trying to enchant her, that bays, coves, and harbors
are for resting only.

And that like her, the universe and St. Anthony all will come home
eventually to you.

O Africans

O Africans
in white dresses
in dark suits
at pleasant evenings.

Singing of the flow
of the sweet Afton
warning of false love
down by the Salley Gardens.

O Africans at quadrille
cutting stately figures
to the lilt of the fiddle
of the fiddle and the bow.

To the melodies of Europe
roll rhythms of the Congo
O Africans imposing bright colors
over the muted tones of Europeans.

Take it all
and turn it around
Slim and Sam for the Salley Gardens
W. B. Yeats for the park downtown.

Add the robust fifth figure
to the stately quadrille
a marriage mixed
but a marriage still.

Sing Africans in white dresses
Cantata Africana
O dark suits sonata, Mento.
Come so now then go so.

O Africans
in white dresses
in dark suits
at pleasant evenings.

Morning, Morning Angel Mine

Four in the morning
you turn me over
to speak into me some new knowledge.

Today's lesson is about life more abundant
and sweet singing
about why we move so
to the kumina of the Congo
"All a we a one Bungo"

Why we sing so to the Yoruba of Brazil
Gilberto, Gil, Nascimento, Jobim
riffing down the lips of a stone flower
wonder which notes register keener
wild woman crying or wild violins.

Mornings with you Cherubim I wake
to hear you whispering all the promises you make
when we are on the earth plane and awake.
Soft in the hours of nectar
you whisper to me of promises kept
and promises keeping.

They fall about us like angel feathers
swept with the lightest of brooms.
Airborne now are our promises
in this lit and sanctified room.

What they cannot see
is that their reality
smokes dimly at the periphery
of us. What we are about is
liquid jewels for wine

Carnelian star apples
ruby bird cherries

celebrations in a sealed space
sacred and divine.
Their striving horns
emit dull sounds and fall
as lusterless still lives.

What we are about
is outside of imagining.
Today's lesson is about
life more abundant and
sweet singing

Golden apples and
sweet cups brimming
spirit rosemary wine

Old wine skins cast off
into the flow
of the regenerating
Rio Nuevo
upon your lips
the taste of new wine

Morning morning
Angel mine.

Bulls Bay, Lucea

Today harvest Sunday
the Parish Church is full
of formal worship.

They have brought in the sheaves
and the bounty is laid
fruitful evidence at the altar.

Ribbon-striped sugar-cane and moon-white yams
is what these parts,
my mother's country, is known for.

An artist among them has strung
bright bulbs of hot ripe peppers
glowing high across the Altar.

The congregation sings
from the hymnal of the Church
of England,
"We plough the fields and scatter."

I walk past the Church
down to the seaside
immersion, deep cleansing
today is what I am after.

Here there is a mother
bathing a young baby.
She is sopping, stretching its limbs
reshaping the pliant body
in the salt water.

A child is building sand structures
testing the texture of the sand
between her fingers.

Sometimes she stops and stares
out to sea
with the liquid eyes of a dreamer.

There is a youth who just emerged
from a one-room
barely high enough to stand in

he is now sitting on the low branch
of a coco plum tree.
He is smoking something.

A woman with a bitter green
body smell
is screaming at three small children
not to venture too far into the water,

which, as if belying her warning
is calm and wears a silver sheen
and laps lovingly at the shoreline.

To an observer this is a perfect
watercolor,
"Natives bathing in a benign sea,"
and the waves speak a timeless sermon

say
that all flesh is grass

say
that the only thing which lasts
is something that the eye cannot see

say
that it can work mysteriously
in the hearts of women and men

say
that it can change the plans of them
who do not count these women and these men.

[67]

The one sopping the limbs of the baby
so that it will be strong in the joints
to take life's blows.

The youth smoking something
so that the roof of his room can touch the skies
in imitation of the mercurial rise
of his dreams.

The bitterbush woman
screaming at the children
who want to run away from that voice,
sounding strident warnings repeatedly
about shark danger lurking
beneath calm seas.

And the small dreamer
wishing that she could walk upon water
across to cities of tall solid structures,
real pepper lights
but no warm watercolor sea.

Far from Bulls Bay, Lucea
where I worship, adding my salt to the sea,
repeating after the sermon of the waves

say
All flesh is grass

say
The only thing that lasts
is the enigma of a leaven
the eye cannot see . . .

say
As I baptize myself
with these people today
say
Lord have mercy on me.

To Us, All Flowers Are Roses

Accompong is Ashanti, root, Nyamekopon.
Appropriate name, Accompong, meaning
warrior or lone one. Accompong,
home to bushmasters, bushmasters being
maroons, maroons dwell in dense places
deep mountainous well sealed
strangers unwelcome. Me No Send You No Come.

I love so the names of this place
how they spring brilliant like "roses"
(to us all flowers are roses), engage you
in flirtation. What is their meaning? Pronunciation?
A strong young breeze that just takes
these names like blossoms and waltz
them around, turn and wheel them on the tongue.

There are angels in St. Catherine somewhere.
Arawak is a post office in St. Ann.
And if the Spaniards hear of this
will they come again in Caravelles
to a post office (in suits of mail)
to inquire after any remaining arawaks?
Nice people, so gentle, peaceful, and hospitable.

There is everywhere here.
There is Alps and Lapland and Berlin.
Armagh, Carrick Fergus, Malvern
Rhine and Calabar, Askenish
where freed slaves went to claim
what was left of the Africa within
staging secret woodland ceremonies.

Such ceremonies! such dancing, ai Kumina!
drum sound at Barking Lodge where we hear
a cargo of slaves landed free, because
somebody sign a paper even as they

[69]

rode as cargo shackled on the high seas.
So they landed here, were unchained, went free.
So in some places there is almost pure Africa.

Some of it is lost, though, swept away forever,
maybe at Lethe in Hanover, Lethe springs
from the Greek, a river which is the river
of Oblivion. There is Mount Peace here
and Tranquility and Content. May Pen
Dundee Pen, Bamboo Pen and for me,
Faith's Pen, therefore will I write.

There is Blackness here which is sugar land
and they say is named for the ebony of the soil.
At a wedding there once the groom wore cobalt blue
and young bride, cloud white, at Blackness.
But there is blood, red blood in the fields
of our lives, blood the bright banner flowing
over the order of cane and our history.

The Hope River in hot times goes under,
but pulses underground strong enough to rise
again and swell to new deep, when the May rains
fall for certain. There was a surfeit once
of Swine in Fat Hog quarter and somehow
Chateau Vert slipped on the Twi of our tongue
and fell to rise up again as "Shotover."

They hung Paul Bogle's body at sea
so there is blood too in the sea, especially
at Bloody Bay where they punctured balloons
of great grey whales. There is Egypt here
at Catadupa, a name they spoke first softly
to the white falling cataracts of the Nile.
There is Amity and Friendship and Harmony Hall.

Stonehenge . . . Sevens, Duppy Gate, Wait a Bit,
Wild Horses, Tan and See, Time and Patience,
Unity. It is Holy here, Mount Moses

dew falls upon Mount Nebo, south of Jordan,
Mount Nebo, rises here too hola Mount Zion high.
Paradise is found here, from Pisgah we look out
and Wait a Bit, Wild Horses, Tan and See, Time and Patience, Unity.

For the wounded a Doctor's Cave
and at Phoenix Park from Burnt Ground new rising.
Good Hope, the mornings dawn crystalline
at Cape Clear. It is good for brethren
and sistren to dwell together in Unity
on Mount Pleasant. Doctor Breezes issue from the side
of the sea across parishes named for saints.

Rivers can be tied together in eights.
Mountains are Lapis Lazuli or Sapphire,
impossibly blue, and rivers wag their waters
or flow Black or White or of Milk.
And the waters of the Fish River do contain
and will yield up, good eating fish. O heart
when some nights you cannot sleep,

for wondering why you have been charged
to keep some things of which you cannot speak,
think what release will mean, when your name
is changed to Tranquility. I was born at Lineen—
Jubilee!—on the anniversary of Emancipation Day.
I recite these names in a rosary, speak them
when I pray, for Heartease, my Mecca, aye Jamaica.

Trident

Entering Hope Bay, you begin to sense
at the same time that you sight the sea
that this division of the world's waters
into five or so oceans and seven seas
is just some cartographer's divisive dream.
All salt waters run without boundary
into each other, their volume helped
by earth's fresh rivers
who abandon their running ways finally
into the saline life of the one body.

I sit in Paradise, even as I write
facing this view of what I now conclude
is the world's one body of water.
It is foaming, churning so against the rocks
which at this point are called honeycomb,
that is, before they are broken down finally
into what will then be called rock honey,
sliding down to coat the sea's side
providing nutrient rich feeding walls
for the world's fish.

So sing today of the unity of all things.
How everything comes eventually home.
The bright peacocks share my early breakfast,
the coronetted white one feeds
upon shards of icy food which have fallen
from last night's full moon.
Within the blackbird's feathers glow
all colors, but you have to have the eye
and to trust the second layer of sunlight
in order to truly see them.

I turn and turn in wonder, who could have put
all this together?

The same hand that is forever reconciling
all things.
In the workings of the most mighty economy
our gifts and needs fit.

Balance this upon the only principle that abides,
and bless it.
So I'll accept all of this then, the morning,
the breakfast, the peacocks on the terrace.

Accept the sea the salt the bread.
May the peace within this poem
stay the devils in our heads.

Out of the blackbird's feathers shine
the holy peacock blue.
All things, all things work together.

Furnace Harbor: A Rhapsody of the
North Country
Philip D. Church (1988)

Bad Girl, with Hawk
Nance Van Winckel (1988)

Blue Tango
Michael Van Walleghen (1989)

Eden
Dennis Schmitz (1989)

Waiting for Poppa at the Smithtown
Diner
Peter Serchuk (1990)

Great Blue
Brendan Galvin (1990)

What My Father Believed
Robert Wrigley (1991)

Something Grazes Our Hair
S. J. Marks (1991)

Walking the Blind Dog
G. E. Murray (1992)

The Sawdust War
Jim Barnes (1992)

The God of Indeterminacy
Sandra McPherson (1993)

Off-Season at the Edge of the World
Debora Greger (1994)

Counting the Black Angels
Len Roberts (1994)

Oblivion
Stephen Berg (1995)

To Us, All Flowers Are Roses
Lorna Goodison (1995)

Honorable Amendments
Michael S. Harper (1995)

Points of Departure
Miller Williams (1995)

NATIONAL POETRY SERIES

Eroding Witness
Nathaniel Mackey (1985)
Selected by Michael S. Harper

Palladium
Alice Fulton (1986)
Selected by Mark Strand

Cities in Motion
Sylvia Moss (1987)
Selected by Derek Walcott

The Hand of God and a Few Bright
Flowers
William Olsen (1988)
Selected by David Wagoner

The Great Bird of Love
Paul Zimmer (1989)
Selected by William Stafford

Stubborn
Roland Flint (1990)
Selected by Dave Smith

The Surface
Laura Mullen (1991)
Selected by C. K. Williams

The Dig
Lynn Emanuel (1992)
Selected by Gerald Stern

My Alexandria
Mark Doty (1993)
Selected by Philip Levine

The High Road to Taos
Martin Edmunds (1994)
Selected by Donald Hall

Theater of Animals
Samn Stockwell (1995)
Selected by Louise Glück

OTHER POETRY VOLUMES

Local Men and *Domains*
James Whitehead (1987)

Her Soul beneath the Bone: Women's
Poetry on Breast Cancer
Edited by Leatrice Lifshitz (1988)

Days from a Dream Almanac
Dennis Tedlock (1990)

Working Classics: Poems on Industrial
Life
Edited by Peter Oresick and Nicholas Coles
(1990)

Hummers, Knucklers, and Slow
Curves: Contemporary Baseball Poems
Edited by Don Johnson (1991)

The Double Reckoning of Christopher
Columbus
Barbara Helfgott Hyett (1992)

Selected Poems
Jean Garrigue (1992)

New and Selected Poems, 1962–92
Laurence Lieberman (1993)

The Dig and *Hotel Fiesta*
Lynn Emanuel (1994)

For a Living: The Poetry of Work
Edited by Nicholas Coles and Peter Oresick
(1995)